# APEX

## HOW TO WORK FROM HOME AND MAKE 6 FIGURES AS AN APEX PROGRAMMER

TENS OF THOUSANDS OF
PEOPLE HAVE BECOME
SALESFORCE DEVELOPERS
HERE'S HOW
YOU CAN TOO

**ADAM PARKER**

ISBN: 978-1-7352298-6-7

Front cover design by Adam Parker

First printing edition 2020.

parkertechconsulting.com

# Table of Contents

## Introduction

Most people think writing code and doing development work is hard. Well, it can be... if you make it hard. However, like most things there are patterns; reusable blocks that you can apply from other methodologies to make things easier and learn things at a much quicker pace.

Apex is a very powerful language. Similar to Java, PHP and others you can use Apex to do just about anything. Additionally, you are also connected to the leading Software As A Service (SAAS) platforms in the world (Salesforce.com), which is one of the most powerful content management systems on the market. This combination makes learning and knowing Apex development highly sought after and extremely valuable to you as a developer.

Over the years I've worked for small start-ups, non-profits, government agencies with a lot of red tape as well as large companies working in a team environment. Each one has its positive and negatives and some pay well and some not much at all. However, through each experience I've been able to become a better developer by continuing to code, continuing to learn, continuing to put the rubber to the road and deliver top quality outcomes for the customers I work with.

Whether your goals are to be a developer, architect, consultant or administrator, knowing Apex will take you far and open up opportunities in your career like no other. This book will get you started and give you an incredible edge in jumpstarting your training. The following chapters will walk you through the way that I got started but also show you some of the lessons I've learned and pitfalls to avoid along the way. Being a good developer means not only knowing what you CAN do, but what you CAN'T do as well what you may want to avoid.

Well enough chatting, let's get into it!

*To the love of my life, Stephanie. Thank you for being the most amazing wife and the best friend I could ever ask for. There is no one I would rather sit next to at night and share this journey with.*

## Chapter 1: Understanding Salesforce

If you've been thinking about Salesforce, you aren't alone. It's THE fastest growing cloud platform in the world. The first thing you should do is **Sign up for a FREE Developer Org at https://developer.salesforce.com/signup.** Salesforce allows you to sign up for your own developer org where you can begin to learn Salesforce. To really understand the topics we will cover in this book and begin to start learning Salesforce, you need to see it in action. As you go through this book, I recommend trying some of these things for yourself.

Salesforce is one of the most popular cloud platforms in the business world, arguably THE most popular. It is definitely one of the fastest growing sectors in the tech industry. Businesses are flocking to put their data into Salesforce and are hiring Salesforce Administrators, Salesforce Developers, Salesforce Architects and more to help take their businesses to new levels using this amazing platform.

This is where we come in. This book is geared toward the developer or those aspiring to be a developer. In this chapter we will cover some of the basics of Salesforce that are important to understand to help build a framework for some of the future concepts we will discuss in this book.

If you already have some experience in Salesforce, or are already a Salesforce Administrator then you may want to skip to the next chapter.

However, if you are just getting started with Salesforce or are at the beginning of your Salesforce journey, then there are a few things you want to get under your belt to help you succeed as a developer.

## Powerful Cloud-based CRM

So what is Salesforce? Salesforce is a cloud-based CRM (Customer Relationship Management). This online platform is responsible for managing a business' relationships and interactions with customers and potential customers. With a CRM businesses can stay connected to customers, streamline processes, and improve their profitability.

There are so many moving pieces to a business such as sales, leads, marketing, customer service, social media monitoring, etc. A CRM system for a business can provide a clear overview of a business through the use of Dashboards, Reports and Views of Accounts, Contacts and more.

## Objects, Fields, Records & Tabs

In Salesforce data is categorized into Objects and Fields. An object is like a table like you would see in a spreadsheet like excel. A field is like a column on that spreadsheet that has a header name to it. Each row in that spreadsheet would be considered a "Record" in salesforce.

If you think about it like a spreadsheet with columns and rows, it's pretty easy to understand the basic structure of Salesforce. Now obviously that structure and architecture can get quite a bit more complex depending on what you want to do with the data.

One of the foundational components of how Salesforce works is how Salesforce objects, fields and data are related to each other.

For example, let's take the Accounts and Contacts objects. These two objects are related to teach other in a parent-child relationship; Accounts is the parent object and Contacts are the child object. An Account can have many child Contacts associated with it. Pretty easy stuff right?

When you log into Salesforce you will notice the menu across the top of the page. The objects in Salesforce are displayed in this menu through the use of what Salesforce calls "Tabs." You can add or remove these Tabs as you see fit and customize your instance of Salesforce from within Salesforce Setup. We will discuss Salesforce Setup shortly.

## Standard & Custom Objects

There are two types of objects in Salesforce, Standard and Custom. Salesforce comes out of the box with many Standard objects. Objects such as Accounts, Contacts, Cases and Opportunities are commonly used Standard objects. You can also create Custom Objects. A Custom Object is a user created object that you can use for tracking data that is not available out of the box for Salesforce.

The power of Salesforce comes from it's ability to be customized. This customization starts with the custom objects and custom fields, but doesn't end there. The ability to create custom automations easily through point and click as well as through code is one of the reasons Salesforce is the leader in the cloud-based CRM world.

## Salesforce Classic vs. Salesforce Lightning

There are two main views or "experiences" of Salesforce: Salesforce Classic and Salesforce Lightning. Classic is the old school view and Lightning is the newer more updated view. As you interact more with Salesforce you will see both of these options. As of this book, I would recommend starting and sticking with Lightning as that is where all of the new updates and development from Salesforce is happening.

## Salesforce Setup

Then there is Salesforce Setup. Salesforce Setup is a powerful tool that allows you to set up, maintain and customize your instance of Salesforce however you desire. You will be using Salesforce Setup frequently as a Developer or Administrator.

To access Salesforce Setup, look at the top of any page. Depending on the view or experience of Salesforce you are using, In lightning you will see a ⚙ gear icon, where you can click Setup Home. If you are using   Classic  you   will   see   a Setup link.

## Chapter 2: Understanding Developer Console

Salesforce has a development environment that is built right into the online Salesforce.com platform. It provides the ability to write code, debug your code and test the code you've written. Additionally, you can write queries using the "Query Editor" or review logs when troubleshooting codes.

Open the developer console and you will see 3 sections on the screen. At the top is the menubar, in the middle is the main workspace and at the bottom are your logs, tests, query editor and problems panel.

### Log Inspector

Within the Developer Console, one of the most common things I do as a developer is to use the log inspector for debugging code. Whenever any operation happens it shows up in the log inspector. This area is a context-sensitive execution viewer that shows the source of an operation, what triggered the operation, as well as any events that happened next. While using this tool we can analyze database events, Apex code execution, validation logic and any other processes that occur.

Within these debug logs a common use is to use it to debug code when errors occur. When an error occurs you are able to view the error as well as the line of code where the error occurred for enhanced troubleshooting.

## Query Editor

The developer console also includes a powerful query editor. This allows you to write and execute SOQL and SOSL queries on data currently in the Salesforce org. This is very helpful for testing queries to ensure you are getting the proper results before placing it in your Apex code. You can also use this for troubleshooting problematic queries when you are experiencing errors in your code.

When you're using the Query editor the query has 3 parts in the screenshot above:

    1. SELECT Id

    2. FROM Account

    3. WHERE Name Like 'Test%'

Unlike other SQL languages, you can't use * to retrieve all fields. You must be specific for every field you want to return. If you try to access a field you haven't specified in the query, you will get an error.


**Generate and Analyze Logs**

Debug logs are the life blood of testing and troubleshooting Apex in Salesforce. Anytime you execute any Apex code you are able to see the results in the logs. You can use the logs to debug your code by adding user defined debug statements in specific parts of your code to make sure your queries are returning the results you are expecting and your code is functioning properly.

You can view debug logs from 2 different areas in Salesforce. The first area is in the developer console. When you open up the developer console, the first tab in the bottom section is the logs tab. The second area where you can view debug logs is by going to Salesforce Setup and searching for "Debug logs" in the quick find search. When you click on debug logs, this pulls up a page that allows you to not only view logs, but setup trace flags on other Salesforce users so you can view logs for yourself or logs that are not your own. This is available only on this page as developer console only allows you to view your own logs.

There are some limitations to debug logs you may want to know about and you can find out more about those limitations in Salesforce Help under "Set Up Debug Logging".

As an Apex developer within Salesforce, you will want to be aware of how your code is affecting the Salesforce Governor Limits. Because Salesforce runs in a multi tenant environment, the Apex runtime engine limits are strictly enforced so that runaway Apex code or process don't monopolize shared resources. If your Apex code exceeds a limit, it will through an error and you will need to know what those limits are and how close you are to exceeding those limits.

Debug logs allow also display your limit usage showing you Number of SOQL queries, DML statements, heap size, callouts, etc. You can see in the developer console log below an example of a log that was generated and see that 1 out of 100 SOQL queries were used, 2 out of 10,000 DML statements were used and so on. This is very helpful information to pay attention to.

I'll talk about Apex Coding Best Practices later on in this book so that you can make sure to write your code in an efficient was so as not to exceed these errors and write great code!

# APEX

| Timestamp | Event | Details |
|---|---|---|
| 21:23:17:679 | HEAP_ALLOCATE | [EXTERNAL]|Bytes:8 |
| 21:23:17:747 | DML_END | [56]| |
| 21:23:17:748 | METHOD_EXIT | [33]|01p1Q00000Jr9EF|AccountPDFGenerator.attachPDF(Account, String) |
| 21:23:17:748 | SYSTEM_MODE... | false |
| 21:23:17:748 | METHOD_EXIT | [16]|01p1Q00000Jr9EF|AccountPDFGenerator.generateAccountPDF(Account) |
| 21:23:17:748 | CUMULATIVE_L... | |
| 21:23:17:748 | LIMIT_USAGE_... | (default)| |
| 21:23:16:000 | LIMIT_USAGE_... | Number of SOQL queries: 1 out of 100 |
| 21:23:16:000 | LIMIT_USAGE_... | Number of query rows: 1 out of 50000 |
| 21:23:16:000 | LIMIT_USAGE... | Number of SOSL queries: 0 out of 20 |
| 21:23:16:000 | LIMIT_USAGE_... | Number of DML statements: 2 out of 150 |
| 21:23:16:000 | LIMIT_USAGE_... | Number of DML rows: 2 out of 10000 |
| 21:23:16:000 | LIMIT_USAGE_... | Maximum CPU time: 476 out of 10000 |
| 21:23:16:000 | LIMIT_USAGE_... | Maximum heap size: 0 out of 6000000 |
| 21:23:16:000 | LIMIT_USAGE_... | Number of callouts: 0 out of 100 |
| 21:23:16:000 | LIMIT_USAGE_... | Number of Email Invocations: 0 out of 10 |
| 21:23:16:000 | LIMIT_USAGE_... | Number of future calls: 0 out of 50 |
| 21:23:16:000 | LIMIT_USAGE_... | Number of queueable jobs added to the queue: 0 out of 50 |
| 21:23:16:000 | LIMIT_USAGE_... | Number of Mobile Apex push calls: 0 out of 10 |
| 21:23:16:000 | LIMIT_USAGE_... | |
| 21:23:17:748 | LIMIT_USAGE_... | MC4SF| |
| 21:23:16:000 | LIMIT_USAGE_... | Number of SOQL queries: 0 out of 100 |
| 21:23:16:000 | LIMIT_USAGE_... | Number of query rows: 0 out of 50000 |

☐ This Frame  ☐ Executable  ☐ Debug Only  ☐ Filter  Click here to filter the log

9

## Chapter 3: The Language of Salesforce Coding

### Apex Triggers and Classes

When you first get into Apex development you will start to hear a lot about Triggers and Classes. These may be new words for you or they may seem concepts difficult to grasp, but don't fret, they are easy once you get used to them. Triggers and classes really go hand in hand. Triggers fire after certain operations and act as kind of listeners and classes do the heavy lifting. You will usually find that you call classes inside your triggers.

One important note is that Apex code, whether classes or triggers, cannot be written in a production environment. Apex code must be written in sandbox and then migrated from a sandbox to production. We will go over this more in the chapter on Unit Tests & Code Coverage.

### Triggers

The official salesforce definition of a Trigger is "Apex code that executes before or after the following types of operations: insert; update; delete; merge; upsert; undelete." Now don't worry if you don't know what an upsert or undelete is... the important thing to know is that 1) a Trigger uses Apex code 2) a Trigger executes before or after an operation and 3) Those operations are insert, update, delete (and a few others).

Example of a Simple Trigger:

```
1 ▾ trigger TestTrigger on Account (after insert, after update) {
2        // Do some action here
3 }
```

Let's break the above code down. You start out the trigger by writing "trigger" (which tells you this is a trigger) and then the name of the trigger, which in this case is "TestTrigger". Easy right?

The next part is uses the word "on" (to tell you which object this trigger will be listening for) and then "Account", which is obviously the Account object. What this is saying is that this trigger will work specifically with actions the happen to the Account object. The trigger is basically waiting for some action to occur with the Account object and then it springs into action.

You can access triggers in 3 main places:

1. Setup > Custom Code > Apex Triggers > Here you will see a list of all Triggers.

2. By opening Developer Console > Clicking File > Open > Selecting "Triggers" and here you will see a list of all Triggers.

3. Setup > Objects > Select the Object you want such as Account > Select "Triggers" in the left column list. This will show you all Triggers on a specific object.

**Apex Classes**

Just like in Java, you can create classes in Apex. I like to think of a class as the core or main meat of the operation. In Apex classes, you can create / call methods, create / use variables, for loops, create SOQL and SOSL queries and Create, Update and Delete Salesforce records. For every piece of code in your classes you must also create a test class to provide coverage for that code, but more about that later.

You can access Apex classes in 2 main places:

1. Setup > Custom Code > Apex Classes > Here you will see a list of all Triggers.

2. By opening Developer Console > Clicking File > Open > Selecting "Classes" and here you will see a list of all Classes.

Usually Triggers and Classes go hand in hand. Your Trigger will usually call a method in the Class and then the Class handles the actions and behaviors.

## SOQL, SOSL & DML

Within your classes you will find that you can do things like creating methods, variables and very importantly... interact with Salesforce data / records.

SOQL and SOSL are the two main ways you will interact with the data. SOQL stands for Salesforce Object Query Language and SOSL stands for Salesforce Object Search Language.

If you are familiar with SQL, then SOQL is the equivalent in the Salesforce world. SOQL allows you to create SELECT statements in order to get data and records from the Salesforce database.

SOSL is a programmatic way of interacting with text-based searches against the search index. You will want to use SOSL when you don't know which object or field the data resides in and you want to retrieve data using a keyword search. For text-based searches, SOSL is faster and can return more relevant results.

```
1  List<Account> listAccount = new List<Account>(SELECT Id, Name,
2                                                FROM Account
3                                                WHERE Name = 'Test Account');
```

In the code above, SOQL is being used to get all records from the Account object where Name = 'Test Account'. In this you can see that 2 fields are being returned in the query "Id" and "Name." You can also see that the results of this query are being returned as a List of Accounts with the list name of "listAccount".

You will use SOQL a lot more often than you will use SOSL. Most of the time you will know which objects the data resides in and SOQL will help you retrieve that data from one or more objects that are related to each other.

## DML

The other term you want to be aware of is DML, which stands for Data Manipulation Language. You use DML statements to insert, update, merge, delete and restore data in Salesforce. You will mostly use insert, update and delete.

```
1  Account a = new Account();
2  a.Name = 'New Account';
3  insert a;
```

In the code above, on line 3 is a DML statement to insert a new Account with the name "New Account".

## Batch Processing & Future Methods

Batch Apex is used to perform executions of large jobs that would normally exceed processing limits (think thousands or millions of records). Batch operations run over small batches of records breaking down large tasks into small manageable chunks. These are often called batch jobs. You can write custom batch apex jobs and schedule these jobs to run at specific times.

A future method is a method like a regular method, but it runs in the background, asynchronously. You will often use future methods when using callouts to web services or executing long-running operations. When you call a future method, each future method is queued and executes as system resources are available. One main benefit of using future methods is that some governor limits are higher, such as SOQL query limits and heap size limits. This is especially helpful to know in case you run into these limit errors and need to find a solution to work around these limitations.

You can annotate a method as future by adding the @future text above the method. These methods must be static methods and can only return a void type. I know "static" and "void" types may be new terms as well, so we will cover these in the chapter on Apex Class methods.

## Chapter 4: Triggers

**Types of Triggers**

There are 2 types of triggers. Before triggers and after triggers.

```
1  trigger TestTrigger on Account(before insert, after insert){
2       // Do some action here
3  }
```

This code above uses two different operations that tell you when the code between the brackets { } will fire. These two operations are "before insert" and "after insert". We could have put a number of different operations here, but I chose to go with the most common and simplest ones. You will probably use these two the most often. The first word "before" means that the code within the brackets will only execute BEFORE the insert.

You use "Before" triggers when you want to update or validate record values before they are saved to the database. You use "After" triggers when you want to access data set by the system, such as the Id of a record just inserted, or the DateLastModified of a record.

The full list of operations are insert, update, delete, and undelete.

| | |
|---|---|
| before insert | after insert |
| before update | after update |
| before delete | after delete |
| | after undelete |

15

It's important to note that all classes and triggers must compile successfully and have at least 75% of your Apex code covered by unit tests before you can deploy your code to a production environment.

**Commonly Used Context Variables**

There are some system wide variables that are available for you to use when using triggers. These variables are called context variables because they allow you to access run-time context and are contained within the System.Trigger class.

You can get a full list of these context triggers on the Apex Developer Guide online, however I'm going to give you a few of the commonly used context variables below and why would you use them.

Variables: isInsert, isUpdate, isBefore, isAfter

isInsert and isUpdate variables return true if the trigger was fired due to an insert or update operation. isBefore and isAfter return true if the trigger was fired BEFORE or AFTER any record was saved.

These variables are commonly used in building a Trigger Framework to provide additional conditions so that you can only fire certain methods when a certain condition is true.

```
1  ▾ trigger TestTrigger on Account(before insert, before update, after insert, after update) {
2
3  ▾     if(isInsert && isBefore){
4              // Call beforeInsert method
5          }
6
7  ▾     if(isInsert && isAfter){
8              // Call afterInsert method
9          }
10
11 ▾     if(isUpdate && isBefore){
12             // Call beforeUpdate method
13         }
14
15 ▾     if(isUpdate && isAfter){
16             // Call afterUpdate method
17         }
18
19  }
```

The code above is the start of a Trigger Framework to provide conditions where only certain methods are called and all methods are not run on every execution of this trigger. This is important because it saves on performance time, saves on number of queries being executed and allows you to have full control over which methods are and are not executed.

Variables: `new, newMap, old, oldMap`

`new` returns a list of the new versions of the object's records. `newMap` returns a map of IDs to the new versions of the objects records. `old` returns a list of the old versions of the objects records. `oldMap` returns a map of IDs to the old versions of the objects records.

You would commonly use `new, newMap, old` and `oldMap` when iterating over the lists in a for loop or binding a variable in the IN clause of a SOQL query.

## Calling Class Methods from a Trigger

In a trigger you want to avoid creating methods and putting code logic directly in the trigger. We will cover this more in best practices, but because triggers are optimized to operating in bulk, you want to avoid writing triggers that only deal with one record or that do not account for governor limits.

One of the ways we do this is by limiting logic in our triggers placing our methods in classes. You can then call those methods using the class dot method notation (i.e. `nameOfClass.methodname`). Here is an example below:

```
1 ▾ trigger TestTrigger on Account(before insert){
2
3 ▾     if(isInsert && isBefore){
4           // Call beforeInsert method
5           exampleClass.beforeInsert(trigger.new);
6       }
7
8  }
```

In the code above you can see on line 3, that it is using the isInsert and isBefore to only call this method if the trigger context is before the record has been inserted. It then calls the method named "beforeInsert" from the class named "exampleClass". You can observe above that I am using the "trigger.new" context variable from the trigger class. What this is doing is passing the list of new records to the beforeInsert method so that this method can then make use of this list of records.

## Chapter 5: Apex Classes

If you have experience with other programming languages you will find Apex classes very familiar. It is similar to C# or Java and extremely powerful. However, even if you aren't familiar with other coding languages, Apex is a great place to start building your foundation in learning to code.

I'm not going to cover Apex classes in a comprehensive way, but will unpack what I've found to be the most common use cases I've used and have seen used in day-to-day business use cases.

We introduced the Apex class to you in Chapter 3, but let's unpack this a little further. I'll show you a quick and easy way to create and call an Apex Class.

To create an Apex Class open Developer Console > Click File > New > Apex Class > Enter a name for the new class and click enter. The result is below.

```
1 ▾ public class AccountClass {
2   |
3   }
```

A class can be public, private, global and protected, these are called Access Modifiers. The most commonly used are public and private. Public means the methods or variables in this class can be used by any Apex in this application or namespace. Private, which is the default, means that the method or variable can only be used in this application and cannot be called by any outside Apex classes.

Global means that any method or variable can be used by any other Apex code that has access to the class. A common use for this would be when you are using it in a SOAP API for access from outside salesforce. In order to declare a method or variable as global you also have to declare class as global as well. You will want to use the global modifier rarely because of how it provides limited security and the cross-dependencies are difficult to maintain.

**Class Methods**

Let's talk about Apex methods. In a class you can create one or more methods. You can use these methods do many different things. You can create methods to get records, to insert or update data or to launch a batch process. The great thing is that you get to decide what you want the method to do.

```
1  ▼ public class AccountClass {
2
3  ▼      public String getAccountName(){
4              // Declare
5              String accountName = 'Apple';
6
7              return accountName;
8          }
9
10  }
```

This method "getAccountName" returns a String called accountName with the value of "Apple".

A method can return a value or it can just complete an action and not return any value. If a method returns a value you must declare the type of value it will return. The example above returns a string value.

```
1 ▼ public class AccountClass {
2
3 ▼     public static void insertAccount(){
4           Account a = new Account();
5           a.Name = 'New Account';
6           insert a;
7       }
8
9   }
```

The method above does not return a variable so uses void stating that it will execute but not return a value. Common scenarios you will use void methods will be when inserting, updating or deleting records.

You will also see that I used the term "static". Don't worry too much about that. You can find a detailed explanation in the help online, but just know that you will usually need it when creating methods in order to save time, steps and code later on when calling the method outside of the class.

## Data Types

In order to understand variables you need to have an understanding of Data Types. In Apex, all variables have a data type. This data type can be a salesforce object referred to as an sObject (such as an Account, Contact, etc), it can be a primitive

(String, Integer, Date, DateTime, Id, Boolean, etc), or it can be a Collection (i.e. List (or array), a set of primitives, a map.

Knowing and understanding these different data types is important and is strictly enforced. When you compile your code in order to save it, an error will be thrown if, for example, you assigned an Integer value to a variable with the data type of String.

## Working with Variables

I'll start with a few of the foundations you should know regarding variables to get you started. Just like with Java, variables must be declared and initialized. You can declare one variable at a time or declare multiple variables at a time. See below:

```
1 ▾ public class AccountClass {
2
3       Integer a;
4       Integer d, e, f;
5       Integer i = 0;
6       String myString = 'test string';
7       Boolean b = true;
8
9   }
```

Each line above show different ways to declare and initialize variables.

You can use assignment statements to place values into variables. You have to be aware of data types and the particular way the data type takes the assignment in order to avoid errors.

A simple variable can be assigned as in the example below:

```
1  String s = 'my string';
2  Integer i = 0;
```

## Collections (Lists, Sets, Maps)

Apex uses collections to store multiple records. It's basically just a way to collect records for use later on in your code. You will want to use those records in various ways and you have three different types of collections you can store the records in. Each method has it's own benefits and drawbacks, but you will probably use them all, so it's good to become familiar with them.

## Working with Lists

A list is an ordered collection that can store records of primitive types (integer, string, etc), collection types (lists, sets, maps), sObjects (Account, Contact, etc), user defined types, and built-in Apex types. Lists CAN have duplicate records.

| Index 0 | Index 1 | Index 2 | Index 3 |
|---|---|---|---|
| 'Ford' | 'Chevrolet' | 'Honda' | 'Toyota' |

In the table above you can see a visual representation of a list of strings. The first element in a list is always at position zero

(0). This was a list of strings, but a list can be a list of lists, and be multidimensional.

In order to use a list, you must declare it using the keyword `List` followed by the type of list you will be using.

```
1  List<String> listOfCarMakes = new List<String>();
2  System.debug('List of Car Makes: ' + listOfCarMakes);
```

Above you can see that I created a list of strings called "listOfCarMakes". On line 2 I am printing out the values that are in the list to help with debugging. Currently this would not print out any values since we have only declared and instantiated the list, but not added any values to it.

Lets add 4 cars to the list as in our example on the previous page.

```
1  List<String> listOfCarMakes = new List<String>();
2  System.debug('List of Car Makes: ' + listOfCarMakes);
3
4  listOfCarMakes.add('Ford');
5  listOfCarMakes.add('Chevrolet');
6  listOfCarMakes.add('Honda');
7  listOfCarMakes.add('Toyota');
8
9  System.debug('List of Car Makes: ' + listOfCarMakes);
```

You can add values to the list using the above notation and then when you print out the debug value, you will see the 4 cars now in the list.

It's also possible to add values to the list in a different way using less code. I'm all for using less code when possible because it usually makes things simpler and easier to understand.

```
1  List<String> listOfCarMakes = new List<String>{
2              'Ford', 'Chevrolet', 'Honda', 'Toyota'};
3  System.debug('List of Car Makes: ' + listOfCarMakes);
```

The above code does will add the strings to the list in only three lines of code .

## Working with Sets

A set is an unordered collection that can store records of any data type, just like lists. Sets however, CANNOT have duplicate records.

```
1  Set<String> setOfCarMakes = new Set<String>{
2              'Ford', 'Chevrolet', 'Honda', 'Toyota'};
3  System.debug('Set of Car Makes: ' + setOfCarMakes);
```

You will want to use a set vs. a list when you need to make sure your collection does not have any duplicate elements. You can add elements to a set using the `.add()` method just like with lists.

## Working with Maps

A map is a collection of key value pairs which contain unique keys for each single value. Keys and values can be of any data type, just like lists and sets.

Below is a table that visually represents a map.

| Car (Key) | 'Ford' | 'Honda' | 'Toyota' |
| --- | --- | --- | --- |
| Car (Value) | 'Mustang' | 'Accord' | 'Corolla' |

With maps you declare it by using the keyword `Map` followed by the data type of both the key and the value.

```
1   Map<String, String> mapOfCars = new Map<String, String>();
2   mapOfCars.put('Ford', 'Mustang');
3   mapOfCars.put('Honda', 'Accord');
4   mapOfCars.put('Toyota', 'Corolla');
5   System.debug('Map of Cars: ' + mapOfCars);
```

You can see that in order to add elements to a map you have to use the keyword `put` vs. `add`. Another different between maps vs. lists and sets is that you add both a key and a value, versus just adding one value to a list or set.

Maps are VERY powerful and whenever I can I try to use maps instead of lists when it makes sense.

We will be talking more about lists, sets and maps in the next section dealing with For Loops and SOQL queries. There we will see how to put query results into these collections and then access their values inside for loops.

**Working with SOQL Queries**

When working with lists you will often need to write a query and put the results in a list or a map. One of the tasks I find myself doing very often is when working in an after trigger, taking the trigger.new list, looping through the list to get a set of ids, then doing a query on that set of ids and putting it into a map. I'll show you an example.

```
 1 ▾ trigger TestTrigger on Account (after insert, after update) {
 2      // Declare set variable
 3      Set<Id> setOfAccountIds = new Set<Id>();
 4
 5      // Loop through trigger.new list and add accountids to Set
 6 ▾    for(Account a :trigger.new){
 7          setOfAccountIds.add(a.Id);
 8      }
 9
10      // Get contacts from query and create a map of contacts
11      Map<Id, Contact> mapContacts = new Map<Id, Contact>(
12                      [SELECT Id FROM Contact
13                      WHERE accountId IN :setOfAccountIds]);
14 }
```

## Working with For Loops

We have used a few for loops in some previous examples, but lets take a moment to understand the value of for loops. There are three different types of loops available in Apex, the for loop, the do while loop and the while loop. We will focus on the for loop since it will be the one most commonly used.

For loops are basically blocks of code that you can execute over and over again until a certain condition is met. You will usually execute for loops on lists, but you can also execute them on sets. Here examples of the three types of for loops you can execute in Apex.

```
 1 ▾ trigger TestTrigger on Account (after insert, after update) {
 2      // Traditional for loop
 3 ▾    for(Integer i = 0; i < 200; i++){
 4          // do something
 5      }
 6      // SOQL for loop
 7 ▾    for(Account a : [SELECT Id FROM Account]){
 8          // do something
 9      }
10      // List or set iteration of a for loop
11 ▾    for(Account a :Trigger.new){
12          // do something
13      }
14 }
```

27

### Creating, Updating & Deleting Records

One of the most common use cases, if not THE most common use case for using triggers and Apex code is to modify Salesforce records. Salesforce has it's own specific way of working with their records called DML (Data Manipulation Language). DML is basically a series of keywords you utilize to modify records in Salesforce.

It's important to know how DML works and how to stay within the boundaries set in place by Salesforce so that you don't run into any DML governor limits.

You can perform DML on either a single object or bulk objects. To avoid hitting DML limits, such as 150 DML statements per transaction, bulk processing of records is the recommended way. When you perform a DML statement on a list it only counts as one DML statement.

The following are the DML statements available to use: `insert`, `update`, `upsert`, `delete`, `undelete` and `merge`. Apex also contains built-in database methods. These methods allow more granular control of data manipulation including the ability to specify whether an operation should partially succeed or not. These methods are:

- `Database.insert()`
- `Database.update()`
- `Database.upsert()`
- `Database.delete()`
- `Database.undelete()`
- `Database.merge()`

The below example shows a how NOT to perform a DML operation.

```
1 ▾ trigger TestTrigger on Account (after insert, after update) {
2       |
3 ▾     for(Account a :trigger.new){
4           Contact c = new Contact();
5           c.FirstName = 'John';
6           c.LastName = 'Doe';
7           insert c;
8       }
9   }
```

If you place an update inside a for loop you put your code at risk of throwing errors and not executing properly because it will very likely hit the DML limit.

The recommended way to perform an insert of a new record would be using a list as in the example below.

```
1 ▾ trigger TestTrigger on Account (after insert, after update) {
2
3       List<Contact> newContactToInsert = new List<Contact>();
4
5 ▾     for(Account a :trigger.new){
6           Contact c = new Contact();
7           c.FirstName = 'John';
8           c.LastName = 'Doe';
9           newContactToInsert.add(c);
10      }
11
12      insert newContactToInsert;|
13  }
```

You can see that the `insert` statement is outside of the for loop which means it will only get executed one time. However, the "newContactToInsert" list is using the `.add()` method and will get called during each loop. Pretty cool huh?

I've showed you how to insert a record, but let's look at updating a record. In order to update a record you need to have the id of record you are going to update. This is so that you can make sure that you are updating the right record. See the example below:

```
1  ▼ trigger TestTrigger on Account (after insert, after update) {
2
3       List<Account> updateAccount = new List<Account>();
4
5  ▼    for(Account a :trigger.new){
6           a.Name = 'New Account Name';
7           updateAccount.add(a);
8       }
9
10      update updateAccount;
11  }
```

You can easily delete records in Apex by executing the following code:

```
1  ▼ trigger TestTrigger on Account (after insert, after update) {
2
3       List<Account> deleteAccount = new List<Account>();
4
5  ▼    for(Account a :trigger.new){
6  ▼        if(a.Name == 'Test Account'){
7               deleteAccount.add(a);
8           }
9       }
10
11      delete deleteAccount;
12  }
```

## Chapter 6: Unit Tests & Code Coverage

In Salesforce, all apex code must be covered by test code before the code can be migrated to a production environment. Apex code cannot be directly written into a production environment and must be deployed. In order to deploy your Apex classes and triggers, you must write test classes.

These test classes ensure that your Apex code works as expected and also provide you with regression tests that can be rerun each time your classes and triggers are updated ensuring the integrity of your existing functionality. The test classes also have to meet a minimum code coverage requirements.

### Code Coverage Requirements for Deployment

In order for you to deploy your code to a production environment you will need to make sure your test classes "cover" your Apex code with a required minimum of 75% code coverage. 100% is always better, but Salesforce requires at least 75%.

Your test coverage should not only be written just to meet this code coverage requirement. Test classes, or Unit Tests, should be written in such a way to test common use cases for your app. This should include both positive and negative tests as well as bulk and single-record processing.

### Writing Your First Unit Test

When writing your first unit test it's good to start from a common framework. The code below is a template I created that I use over and over to start out my unit tests.

```
1    @isTest
2    public class Class_UT {
3
4        public static testmethod void testClass_UT(){
5
6            // Create initial variables
7
8            // Setup Test Data
9            for(Integer i = 0; i < 200; i++){
10
11           }
12
13           Test.startTest();
14
15           Test.stopTest();
16
17           // Create assert statement to verify results
18           // System.assertEquals(200, [SELECT count()
19           //                            FROM Table
20           //                            WHERE Id IN : listIds], 'Error Message: ');
21
22       }
23
24   }
```

Let's break this down a bit.

@isTest: You want to use this to denote that this is a test class and you are using test methods. Test methods must be defined in test classes.

The code above starts out by saying this is a public class with the name "Class_UT". The first and only method in this test class is a method called "testClass_UT" denoted by the line public static testmethod void testClass_UT(). This method uses the keyword void because the method will not return a value.

You can see there is a comment that says // Create initial variables. This is a placeholder where you will create some initial variables to use later on in the code.

You then want to setup your test data and loop through the test data in order to bulkify your test to handle the cases where more than one record may come into your app at at time. This particular for loop is checking for 200 records. 200 records should be a standard test for testing bulk processing since that is also how many records are usually processed at a time through scheduled batch jobs. We will not be looking at batch jobs in this book, but it is good to be aware of them.

`Test.startTest()` and `Test.stopTest()` are two system test methods that you want to use in order to delimit a block of code to get a fresh set of governor limits. Using these delimiters and placing the code you want to test inside of these two methods will isolate the data setup's limit usage.

Next you can see that I have commented out code relating to creating an assert statement to verify results.

`System.assertEquals()` is a system method that helps you to verify your results. The method takes two parameters. The first parameter is the expected value, in this case 200. The second parameter is the actual value. You can find the actual value usually by doing a query after your code has run to verify the results.

**Running Your Tests**

Once your unit test has been written, you are ready to run/ execute your tests. You run your tests using developer console. Open developer console. In the menu click "Test" > "New Run" and then search for the test class by name. Once you find the text class, click on the test class and you will see the name of your test methods in the center window. Click the checkbox next to the test methods you want to run and then click the "Run" button in the lower right hand corner.

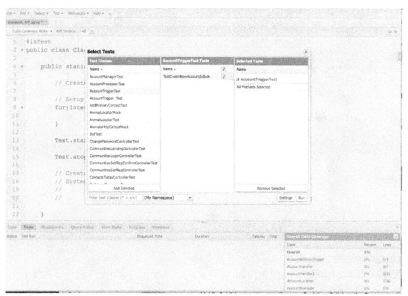

Once you run the test you will get a result in the "Tests" tab down at the bottom of the developer console.

You can see that the status in the test above has a red x. This is stating that the test has a failure. You can then click on the failure to review what the error was and then go back into your test class or your trigger and change the code to fix the error.

## Checking Code Coverage

Once your Test Run passes successfully you will get a green check. Once this happens you are ready to check your code coverage to see how much of your code has been covered and if you are good to go or if you need to include more code in your test class to cover your Trigger / Class Apex code.

```
File ▾   Edit ▾   Debug ▾   Test ▾   Workspace ▾   Help ▾   <   >

ParkLocator.apxc ✕    ParkLocatorTest.apxc ✕

  Code Coverage: None  ▾ | API Version:  48  ✓

 ●  None                        haring class ParkLocator {

    All Tests

    ParkLocatorTest.testCallout 100%  atic String[] country(String c){
    4                             String[] parkNames;
    5                             ParkService.ParksImplPort parks = new Par
    6                             parkNames = parks.byCountry(c);
    7
    8                             return parkNames;
    9             }
    10    }
```

You can check your code coverage by clicking on the "Code Coverage" button on the top left under the file name. There you will find the percentage of coverage that your test class provides for the Apex class.

Additionally, you can check the "Overall Code Coverage" section when you are on the "Test" tab in the bottom right hand side of the developer console. This will provide you with a full list of all classes in your org and you can check there for the percent code coverage to make sure you are above that 75%.

| Overall Code Coverage | | ≫ |
|---|---|---|
| Class | Percent | Lines |
| OlderAccountsUtility | 0% | 0/5 |
| op_trigger_1 | 0% | 0/5 |
| op_trigger_2 | 0% | 0/6 |
| ParkLocator | 100% | 5/5 |
| ParkService | 100% | 27/27 |
| PostPriceChangeToSlack | 0% | 0/28 |

## Chapter 7: Migrating Your Code to Production

### Outbound and Inbound Change Sets

Once your unit tests have all passed and you have 75% code coverage or greater, you can then begin the process of migrating your code from sandbox to production.

In your sandbox org, you must create an outbound change set in salesforce setup, add the apex triggers, classes and any other dependent fields, object, etc to the change set. If there are any components connected to your app that do not exist in your target org, you will need to make sure you include those in the outbound change set. The deployment will fail if you try to deploy a component that refers to missing component.

You may also want to make sure you migrate permissions and access settings to make sure your users can access the new functionality. An important thing to note is that you cannot change a change set once you upload it.

Change sets can only be sent between an org that is affiliated with a production org. If your sandbox org or your developer org is not affiliated with a production org you will not be able to deploy a change set to the production org.

Once you have created the outbound change set, you click the upload button to upload the change set and select the production org to send the change set to. Once the change set has completed the upload, you can log into your production org and go to your inbound change sets to see the change set listed there.

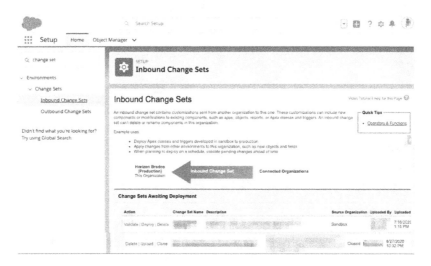

You will then open that inbound change set and validate the change set using test classes. Once it passes validation, you can then deploy the change set into production.

APEX

## Chapter 8: 3 Common Pitfalls to Avoid

**#1 Pitfall To Avoid: Writing Code that is Not Bulkified**

Always write Apex code in a way that can process records in bulk (meaning more than one record at a time). When you write triggers that are bulkified they perform better, consume less server resources and are less likely to hit salesforce platform limits. Your code becomes more able to process large numbers of records with efficiency.

You may think that the only processing that will be done will be from the user interface which only fires one record at a time. However, this thinking fails to take into account other bulk DML calls within other triggers as well as APIs. There may also be customization in the future on your org that is written to use bulk DML calls or APIs that can then trigger bulk actions and your code must be able to handle those calls.

You may also be tested on bulkification on job interviews. This is a very common interview question and knowing how to bulkify your code is a must. Most developers do not know how to write bulkified code, so knowing this will help you to stand out!

One of the primary ways you can bulkify your code is using Maps. Querying your data and placing the results in a map can help prevent you from having to do nested for loops or putting queries inside of for loops.

Below is an example of updating a single record. It's taking the first value in the trigger.new list and assigning it to the variable "a". No matter how many records are in the trigger.new list, this will only update 1 record.

```
1 ▼ trigger on Account(after update){
2       Account a = new Account(trigger.new[0]);
3       a.Name = 'Test Account';
4       update a;
5   }
```

In order to do the same update but in a bulkified way to handle more than 1 record you will need to use a list and a for loop.

```
1 ▼ trigger on Account(after insert){
2       List<Account> accountToUpdate = new List<Account>();
3 ▼     for(Account a :trigger.new){
4           Account newAccount = new Account();
5           newAccount.Name = 'Test Account';
6           accountToUpdate.add(newAccount);
7       }
8       update newAccount;
9   }
```

You can see that there are a few more lines of code to bulkify the code, however this trigger can now handle a bulk data load of records.

#2 Pitfall To Avoid: Queries Inside of For Loops

This is another common thing I see in much of the Apex code I come across, queries inside of for loops. This is a huge concern and will most definitely lead to errors at some point in the future. Sure it may work with a specific test, but once the system starts to be used by your users in a production environment, you can be assured that errors will start to pop up and your code will be buggy. Nobody likes buggy code!

You should also pay attention to where you place your SOQL queries. For instance, there is a 100 SOQL query Salesforce governor limit. If you place a SOQL query inside of a for loop like in the example below, then you put your code at risk of running into a "Too many SOQL queries" error.

```
1 ▾ trigger TestTrigger on Contact (before insert) {
2
3 ▾     for(Contact c : Trigger.new){
4           // if contact phone is blank fill it in with the phone number from the account
5 ▾         if(c.phone == null){
6               Account a = [SELECT phone FROM Account WHERE Id =: c.AccountId];
7               c.phone = a.phone;
8           }
9       }
10
11  }
```

The code above shows BAD code. This for loop contains a SOQL query and is sure to throw an error some point down the road. Let's write this code again, but using a map so that we can get the same data and same result, but bulkify our code.

```
1 ▾ trigger TestTrigger on Contact (before insert) {
2
3       Set<Id> setOfAccountIds = new Set<Id>();
4
5 ▾     for(Contact c : Trigger.new){
6           setOfAccountIds.add(c.AccountId);
7       }
8
9       Map<Id, Account> mapOfAccounts = new Map<Id, Account>([SELECT Id, Phone FROM Account
10                                                 WHERE Id IN :setOfAccountIds]);
11
12 ▾    for(Contact c : Trigger.new){
13          // if contact phone is blank fill it in with the phone number from the account
14 ▾        if(c.Phone == null){
15              c.Phone = MapOfAccounts.get(c.AccountId).Phone;
16          }
17      }
18
19  }
```

What we did here was first, created a set to store a set of AccountIds. We then did a for loop through the list of contacts in the `Trigger.new` list and added the `AccountId` into the `setOfAccountIds`. Next, we created a map that contains an Id as the key and an Account object as the value. We then

41

queried the Account object and put the results in a map. Now we were able to execute the for loop, and access the data in the map using `MapOfAccounts.get(c.AccountId).Phone` instead of writing the query inside of the for loop.

### Bulkifying Your DML

DML statements also need to be bulkified just as SOQL queries do. Because of the shared resource environment of Salesforce there is a 150 DML statement limit. DML statements inside for loops are a big no no. You always want to execute your DML outside of a for loop.

You may feel that you need to loop over a list and execute an update or insert for each record. The way that you can accomplish this requirement yet also make sure your code is going to work in all situations is to use lists.

The code below creates an empty list, loops through a list that's returned from a SOQL query, creates a new Contact and adds that contact to the list called "listOfContacts." The code then inserts that listOfContacts.

```
 1  ▾ trigger on Account(after insert){
 2
 3          List<Contact> listOfContacts = new List<Contact>();
 4
 5          // Use a for loop to create a record and add it to the list
 6  ▾     for(Account a : [SELECT Id FROM Account WHERE id IN :trigger.new]){
 7              Contact newContact = new Contact();
 8              newContact.firstName = 'John';
 9              newContact.lastName = 'Smith';
10              newContact.AccountId = a.Id;
11              listOfContacts.add(newContact);
12          }
13
14          // Execute DML update on list of Contacts
15          insert listOfContacts;
16  }
```

Let's say there were 200 Account records added, then this trigger would have added the contact John Smith to all 200

Account records in 1 DML statement instead of 200; and with no errors!

## #3 Pitfall To Avoid: No Comments

Many say that if your code is written well it shouldn't need comments. That can be true to a point. However, there are many cases where comments are helpful and needed.

I agree that you should definitely write your Apex code in such a way that it is self explanatory and helpful to the reader. Don't write needless comments that just state the obvious or have the tendency to become outdated quickly.

Here are a few commenting practices I recommend.

### The Header Comment:

```
 1 ▼ /**
 2    * @CLASS: Class Name
 3    *
 4    * @DESCRIPTION: This class will do something - provide description
 5    *
 6    *--------------------------------------------------------------------
 7    * DEVELOPER                DATE              REASON
 8    *--------------------------------------------------------------------
 9    * Adam Parker              2020-09-01        created
10    * John Doe                 2020-09-25        Provide update and reason for update
11    ***********************************************************************/
12
```

The header level comment provides a quick snapshot of the purpose of the code. It also provides a way for other developers who come after you to log their modifications as well when any changes are made. This allows you to quickly see a history of the code and who made the changes.

### The Method Comment:
The method comment provides a snapshot of the purpose of the method as well as a history of changes there as well.

```
1 ▾ /**
2   * @trigger: name of trigger that references this method
3   * @description: description of what this method does and why it was created
4   * @author: Adam Parker
5   * <-----CHANGE LOG----->
6   * 2020-09-01 - Created
7   *----------------------------------------------------------------------*/
8
```

Providing this commenting framework will also help other developers to easily log their changes.

Inline comments are usually helpful when you have complex lines of code that need explanation. This could be for for loops, conditions or any difficult to understand code to help provide context. Make sure your comments are short and descriptive, but there is no need to comment each and every statement.

## Chapter 9: Setting Up Your Development Environment

I use Visual Studio Code. It's the development environment that I was first introduced to but also the one that is officially recommended by Salesforce. Many people start out using the Developer Console, which does work but has several limitations. Developer Console works only when online, which prevents you from offline development. However, it really is an essential tool for testing your code. It is also good for making quick changes to your code and working in a single developer environment.

**Download Salesforce Extensions:**

Visual Studio Code offers many Salesforce extensions that are available in the Visual Studio Code Marketplace. One of the main extensions you want to download immediately is the Salesforce Extension Pack. This pack contains seven extensions that will get you started in writing Apex in VS Code.

**Setting Up Your First Project in VS Code:**

Once you have installed the Salesforce Extension Pack you will want to follow the instructions below to setup your first project:

1.  Click on "Add Folder to Workspace"

2.  Navigate to the folder where you want to create your new Workspace and Click Add. This will create your

new workspace.

3. Now enter Control > Shift > P

4. Enter "SFDX: Create Project with Manifest"

5. Choose the folder where you created the project

6. Now enter the name of the project.

7. If you are setting up a development environment, you will need to set the login page to test.salesforce.com in the file "sfdx-project.json".

8. After this you will need to Authorize the org. Click Control > Shift > P to and select "Authorize an Org". This will have you log into the org with your credentials. Once you have done this you are now connected to the org.

9. Now you can right click on the Manifest.xml file, click "Retrieve Source in Manifest From Org".

10. Setup is now complete.

Once you've completed the above steps you have completed the initial setup and are now ready to start creating apex classes, triggers or editing code that's currently on the Salesforce org.

If you work in different Salesforce orgs, you will need to authorize the org from time to time to make sure you are uploading your code to the correct org. I've uploaded my code to the wrong org a time or two and gets a bit frustrating until you figure out that you are connected to the wrong org.

Once you have created your Apex Trigger or your Apex Class and are ready to test, you then just upload the file to the Salesforce org and then test. I enjoy coding in a development environment like this a lot more than coding directly in Developer Console. Once you get used to it you won't want to go back.

There are also so many extensions and plug-ins that can help you code more efficiently that it makes it so worth-while to take the time to learn to use a desktop development environment.

## Chapter 10: Other Resources & Next Steps

I want to take this last chapter and point you to a few of the resources I used along the way to learn to code as well as troubleshoot your projects as you go.

There are so many websites and resources out there, some ok and some great. However, having a systematic approach is not really something that any of them do well.

### Trailhead

I would say that Trailhead (trailhead.salesforce.com) does it the best. However, it can take some time to get through the "trails" because there are so many. Yet it is a superb resource and one I have used and still do use today.

Positives: The great thing about trailhead is it is free to use and hands on learning. They have you spin up a test org and complete tasks in order complete a module. They are broken up into small chunks and you earn badges for each module you complete.

Negatives: Sooo much content it can be overwhelming to know where to start, what to learn, etc. They do break it down into roles, sections, topics, etc, but it's still a lot to take on and it can wear on you.

### Apex Developer Guide

Once you start the path to learning how to write code in Apex, the Apex Developer Guide will be your best friend. This guide will be your reference guide to learning about data types, classes, methods & objects. It gives information on governor limits, more advanced guides to working with exposing Apex Classes as REST Web Services, SOAP Web Services and more.

I use this guide probably weekly in my coding efforts to help make sure I'm calling the right method and making sure my syntax is correct and not going to throw me any errors.

**Workbench**

Another helpful tool is a site called Workbench (workbench.developerforce.com). Workbench is also free to use and allows you to easily view your data and form your queries correctly with it's point and click query editor. It also has a REST explorer that allows you to easily test your web services and APIs.

**Get A Certification**

I probably cannot overstate the value of a Salesforce Certification. Salesforce offers many different certifications such as Salesforce Certified Administrator, Developer, Platform App Builder, and more. Businesses today usually are requiring certifications, so that should be your next step after reading this book. There are Trailhead paths for each type of certification and that is usually a good place to start.

Thank you for giving your time to reading this book. I hope you have found it valuable and I know if you continue with the skills you've learned from this book you will position yourself to be a highly sought after Apex programmer.

**About The Author:**

My name is Adam Parker. I am a Salesforce Technical Architect working at a major silicon valley company. I'm a father to 8 awesome children and my wife is my best friend.

I started Parker Tech Consulting because I have experienced the various ups and downs and difficulties surrounded with getting into the tech industry, what coding language to learn, how to navigate with so many paths. I'm convinced that the Salesforce platform is the where I want to be and want to help people get into Apex coding, become a developer, and land that 6 figure income. Whether that's a job for an amazing tech company or starting your own business, the tech industry for developers is booming.

Join me on this amazing journey.

www.ingramcontent.com/pod-product-compliance
Lightning Source LLC
Chambersburg PA
CBHW061053050326
40690CB00012B/2599